super sad black girl

super sad black girl

diamond sharp

Haymarket Books
Chicago, Illinois

Published in 2022 by
Haymarket Books
P.O. Box 180165
Chicago, IL 60618
773-583-7884
www.haymarketbooks.org
info@haymarketbooks.org

ISBN: 978-1-64259-838-4

Distributed to the trade in the US through Consortium Book Sales and Distribution (www.cbsd.com) and internationally through Ingram Publisher Services International (www.ingramcontent.com).

This book was published with the generous support of Lannan Foundation and Wallace Action Fund.

Special discounts are available for bulk purchases by organizations and institutions. Please email info@haymarketbooks.org for more information.

Cover artwork: "Split Hem" by Angela Davis Fegan
Cover design by Jamie Kerry.

Printed in Canada by union labor.

Library of Congress Cataloging-in-Publication data is available.

10 9 8 7 6 5 4 3 2 1

This book is dedicated to my grandparents, Eugene and Mildred Hill.

"The thing that makes you exceptional, if you are at all, is inevitably that which must also make you lonely."

—Lorraine Hansberry

contents

I

Lorraine and Cognac

I asked you over for a dinner party.
Gwendolyn and Margaret are here too,
but I'm shootin' the shit with you in the corner.
What's it like, dying young?
Having your husband sit shiva for you?
Ms. Hansberry—what happens to Black girls like us?
Do we crust and sugar over our heavy loads?
I'm asking you, Lorraine.
Tell me about the Other Side.
Do Black girls like us get free?
It must be nice over there—
like Chicago with her broken nose,
not easy to love but necessary.
In the purgatory rooms, are Black girls sipping Moscato?
I hope so. Tell me what you want, Lorraine.
I'll bring the Blacks and a bottle of Henny.

Exile

Lorraine and I are sitting in her old apartment in the Village,
two Chicagoans in exile.
She's smoking a Black while I cradle a glass of Henny.
Where can we go to be Black, Ms. Hansberry?
The Other Side? Mars?
I've been thinking about leaving.
Is the only place for Black girls between
the purgatory room and the edge of this universe?

Lorraine takes a long drag and ashes her cigar.

Exile #2

Me and Lorraine are in the Village
sitting in her kitchen.
I say, "I've been thinking about leaving.
I've thought about eating myself whole.
Maybe Black girls get free on the Other Side, Ms. Hansberry."
She lights another Black and takes a long drag.
She say, "Black girls don't get free."

Me and Lorraine are walking through Washington Park.
By the pond, Lorraine takes a drag from a freshly lit Black.
She say, "Black girls have always been free.
We're from the future."

Tired

What if I am tired of myself? What if I am tired of myself?
What if I am tired of myself? What if I am tired of myself?
What if I am tired of myself? What if I am tired of myself?
What if I am tired of myself? What if I am tired of myself?
What if I am tired of myself? What if I am tired of myself?
What if I am tired of myself? What if I am tired of myself?
What if I am tired of myself? What if I am tired of myself?
What if I am tired of myself? What if I am tired of myself?
What if I am tired of myself? What if I am tired of myself?
What if I am tired of myself? What if I am tired of myself?
What if I am tired of myself? What if I am tired of myself?
What if I am tired of myself? What if I am tired of myself?
What if I am tired of myself? What if I am tired of myself?
What if I am tired of myself? What if I am tired of myself?
What if I am tired of myself? What if I am tired of myself?
What if I am tired of myself? What if I am tired of myself?
What if I am tired of myself? What if I am tired of myself?
What if I am tired of myself? What if I am tired of myself?
What if I am tired of myself? What if I am tired of myself?
What if I am tired of myself? What if I am tired of myself?
What if I am tired of myself? What if I am tired of myself?
What if I am tired of myself? What if I am tired of myself?
What if I am tired of myself? What if I am tired of myself?
What if I am tired of myself? What if I am tired of myself?
What if I am tired of myself? What if I am tired of myself?
What if I am tired of myself? What if I am tired of myself?
What if I am tired of myself? What if I am tired of myself?
What if I am tired of myself? What if I am tired of myself?
What if I am tired of myself? What if I am tired of myself?
What if I am tired of myself? What if I am tired of myself?
What if I am tired of myself? What if I am tired of myself?

Purgatory Room

It's me, Sandra, and Rekia in the back of the purgatory room.
I snuck in a bag of Vitner's Crunchy Kurls
and now our fingertips are covered in a dusty red film.
Rekia say she don't remember
the last time she's shot the shit like this.
Everything is fuzzy
and her ears still ring from the buckshot.
Sandra say this is the first fun she's had in this place.

Purgatory Room #2

Me, Rekia, and Sandra are in the back
of the Purgatory Room and this shit's getting boring.
They serve Moscato here and I grab three glasses.
We're Chicago girls—we'll be damned if we don't save ourselves.
Sandra says her neck still hurts and it's hard to swallow.
Her hands have been bloody since the day she came.
Rekia says she has trouble remembering anything before the bullet.

Purgatory Room #3

I'm eating chips drizzled in Louisiana hot sauce.
The only thing good about this place is the snacks.
Rekia says chips were the last thing
she ate before it all went dark.
She and her friends were in the alley shooting the shit.
Then a shot.
Then her head started hurting.
Sandra says she wants to play spades to pass the time.
I don't know how to play.
She invites some guys from the Other Side of the room.
They're from Chicago, too.

Touch

It's up to the living to keep in touch with the dead
It's up to the living to keep in touch with the dead
It's up to the living to keep in touch with the dead

It's up to the living to keep in touch with the dead
It's up to the living to keep in touch with the dead
It's up to the living to keep in touch with the dead

It's up to the living to keep in touch with the dead
It's up to the living to keep in touch with the dead
It's up to the living to keep in touch with the dead

It's up to the living to keep in touch with the dead
It's up to the living to keep in touch with the dead
It's up to the living to keep in touch with the dead

It's up to the living to keep in touch with the dead
It's up to the living to keep in touch with the dead
It's up to the living to keep in touch with the dead

It's up to the living to keep in touch with the dead
It's up to the living to keep in touch with the dead
It's up to the living to keep in touch with the dead

The Golden Shovel

Gwendolyn and I meet for drinks at the Golden Shovel.
The Seven are here and they are shooting pool in the back.

She tells me that the best company are the dead.
They are quiet, agreeable, and make no trouble.

Maud Martha

After the Golden Shovel,
we take a walk on 51st St.
We pass the nacho lady and the ICEE kids,
making our way to the park.
We meet Maud Martha at the lagoon.

Maud Martha is thinking of sending her grandkids
Down South. "It's getting dangerous here."

To be Black means to be in a constant state of migration.

The Other Side

Gwendolyn and I are in Bronzeville, and the sun is shining.
The ghosts that haunt the Golden Shovel come out to chat.
They take us to the back where everyone is smoking.

We both take a drag and Gwendolyn tells me that
the Other Side is just like this one.
The days run longer though
and there's no need for sleep.

We can see the others but they can't see us.
This gives us time to think about things.
There are ports to nearby edges of the Universe.

She tells me that the door to the Black one is just beneath the L.
It's open for the living too. If only they could find it.

Portal

Gwendolyn and I take a walk down the boulevard, to the park.
On the street, we laugh.
Beneath the L stop is the portal, she tells me.
On the Other Side, Black girls are free—whatever that may mean.

Free and Heavy

Lorraine and I meet for lunch.
Gwendolyn and Margaret are here too.
I say, "Is there a point to this?
Does dying always feel so freeing or heavy?"

They look at each other and smile.

Leaving

Lorraine and I meet for lunch.
Gwendolyn and Margaret are here too.
I say, "Is there a point to this?
Why is it so easy to leave?"

All three sigh and say, "We were never really here."

Stay

Lorraine and I take a beat and sit by the drinks.
We are in the land, nowhere, and further from Chicago than we've ever
been.
Gwendolyn joins and tells me to "go the way your blood beats."
What are the things we forget when we cross over?
Do we sing songs of gray?
Does something shatter and fall apart inside?
I am in a process, and I did not come here to stay.
Ms. Brooks says that lasting is not living. I've come this far, why not
stay?

II

Super Sad Black Girl

When I'm tired
I bare my bones.
Swallow my own hair.
Recover from my thoughts.
Drown.
Tweak.
Have a fit of human.
Eat myself whole.
Bleed freely.
Suffocate gleefully.
Drown.
Bury this dust.
Amputate my body.
Abandon my mind.
Cry in public.
Want my ugly.
Choke.
Drown.
Tell the truth.
Fall.
Bleed Black.
Swim in my own blood.
Stay free.
Wander.
Feel entitled.
Stay Black
and die.

Black Girls from the Future

I dream of purgatory rooms that serve whiskey sours.

I want to slit my wrists—vertical not horizontal—I like to be successful.
This is not something you can say in polite conversation.

Fuck polite conversation.

I belong on the moon. The rat done already bit me. I'm rabid. Beam
me up, Sun Ra. Space is the place. Where else can Black girls from the
future go?

The future has been around so long it is now the past. Black girls like
me—where can we go?

Nowhere.

There are hoodoo women, Mississippi clay & tinctures in my blood. Was
born a diviner. Root woman. This is what they called women like me
then. This is my inheritance.

We have always toed the line between the fourth dimension & the Other
Side. There's no place for us now.

No one loves a crazy child. On the Other Side, Black girls are free.

Inheritance

The knocking in my head was cooked in the womb.
(Mississippi folks say that the remedy
for madness in a child is the mother's backchat.)
J. F. K.'s brain blasted
from behind the week my mother's
mother left her newborn shielded
from Chicago winter beside a West Side dumpster.
(The poor girl couldn't bear the chatter of her family.)
The doctor asks whether it runs in the family.

Birthright

I've spent my whole life running from this birthright.
I've spent my whole life running from this birthright.
I've spent my whole life running from this birthright.
I've spent my whole life running from this birthright.
I've spent my whole life running from this birthright.
I've spent my whole life running from this birthright.
I've spent my whole life running from this birthright.
I've spent my whole life running from this birthright.
I've spent my whole life running from this birthright.
I've spent my whole life running from this birthright.

Black Lady Lazarus

Dying is an art and we Black girls do it so well.

Sandra & Korryn & Breonna & Atatiana & Aiyana &
Rekia & Tanisha & Yvette & Miriam & Shelly &
Darnisha & Malissa & Alesia &
Shantel & Shereese & Tarika & Kathryn & Alberta &
Kendra & Natasha & Janisha & Mya & Eleanor &
&&&

Dear Crazy

I vacillate between feeling everything
and nothing at all.
If I told you that you've won
would you leave me alone?

Runaway

My brain taunts me.
It takes twisted satisfaction
in stopping me
in the shower, on the subway.
I'm suicidal more than I'm not.
The silence will kill me if nothing else does.
I'm terrified of people seeing you
and me together,
that they'll run far,
far away from both of us.

Hold On

Sanity is precious.

I highly suggest
holding onto it if one can.

Poppies

I dream of leaving a sea of poppies on my bedroom floor.
My light is deteriorating.

There's nothing
I can do but watch.

Insanity

My insanity is
salve and tincture
co-conspirator
conflicted
judge and jury
like a house with
rooms of grandeur
a home away from home

In Mourning

I'm in constant mourning of my previous self.
   I'm in constant mourning of my previous self.
      I'm in constant mourning of my previous self.
I'm in constant mourning of my previous self.
   I'm in constant mourning of my previous self.
      I'm in constant mourning of my previous self.
I'm in constant mourning of my previous self.
   I'm in constant mourning of my previous self.
      I'm in constant mourning of my previous self.
I'm in constant mourning of my previous self.
   I'm in constant mourning of my previous self.
      I'm in constant mourning of my previous self.
I'm in constant mourning of my previous self.
   I'm in constant mourning of my previous self.
      I'm in constant mourning of my previous self.

Land of the Dead

The entry is located after therapy.
Beneath new prescriptions.
Inside small talk at a bar.
Behind hiding all the knives.
Between incessant travel.
In drafts of suicide notes.
I just can't sit still.

I've been thinking of dying.
Right here and now.

Separation

I'm sitting in my room
with all the lives I can never have.
"I'm fine" is the biggest lie I've ever told.
When the body
separates from the Earth
the first to rush is the blood.
Bitch I'm taking calls,
no small talk.

Room

My room is unkempt.
Suicide would be unkind—
a bother. An inconvenience.
I haven't said goodbye.
I'd have to explain.
It's up to the living to keep in touch with the dead.

Lasting is Not

Lasting is not living. Lasting is not living.
Lasting is not living
Lasting is not living.
Lasting is not living.
Lasting is not living
Lasting is not living. Lasting is not living.
Lasting is not living
Lasting is not living.
Lasting is not living.
Lasting is not living
Lasting is not living. Lasting is not living.
Lasting is not living
Lasting is not living.
Lasting is not living.
Lasting is not living
Lasting is not living. Lasting is not living.
Lasting is not living
Lasting is not living.
Lasting is not living.
Lasting is not living

Never

I can never have all the lives I want.
Where do you go when the truth
is spatchcocked
and flayed?

I Haven't Taken My Medication in Days

What would I do if I were sane?
If my depression lets me outside today?
If dying wasn't an option?

Celebrate

I'm leaving everything except myself.
I'll celebrate the mess.
The deadly.
What can't be accounted for.
Something has shattered and I have fallen into myself.

On the other motherfucking hand, what is a brain?
What is sanity if not tenuous?
What happens when your mind disappears yet remains?
I've spent my whole life running from this birthright.

Only to be crazy anyway.

Inheritance

My illness is an heirloom.

        My illness is an heirloom.

My illness is an heirloom.

      My illness is an heirloom.

        My illness is an heirloom.

My illness is an heirloom.

        My illness is an heirloom.
        My illness is an heirloom.
        My illness is an heirloom.
        My illness is an heirloom.

Affirmations

I made it here from nowhere.
I'm in process.
I did not come here to stay.
It's better to leave alive than dead.

Funerals are for the living.
The dead see themselves out.
Where do the dead go?
What is between that small window between life and death?

It's everywhere and nowhere.

Poppies

I want to slit my wrists.
Cut vertical not horizontal
I strive for perfection in everything I do.
The door to the Other Side exists
in the moment
before the knife hits the vein.
Bleed out.
Float away on a sea of poppies.

The Opening

The opening to the Other Side is beneath the L tracks
next to the beauty supply
(the one that's down next to the corner store).
It is topsy-turvy, discombobulating—
in the way one imagines death may be.
It is no cakewalk.

Take two steps and knock three times.
Take a breath.
Scream.
Rock.
Have a final burst of living.

Ponder.

Release.

Numb

I feel everything and nothing at all.
I feel everything and nothing at all.
I feel everything and nothing at all.
I feel everything and nothing at all.
I feel everything and nothing at all.
I feel everything and nothing at all.
I feel everything and nothing at all.
I feel everything and nothing at all.
I feel everything and nothing at all.
I feel everything and nothing at all.
I feel everything and nothing at all.
I feel everything and nothing at all.
I feel everything and nothing at all.
I feel everything and nothing at all.

The Entry Point Is Visible to Anyone Brave Enough to Look

The entrance is opened
with all of your goodbyes.
Cover the mirrors
Stop the clocks.
Make everything clean.
There is no dying here.

***

Lorraine and I walk past her mural
and step into the alley—
"for a smoke," she says.
It is sunny in Chicago
and we are shooting the breeze before leaving.
"Don't eat too much grief," she says.
"Grief will latch onto you and never leave."
The entrance to the Other Side is just ahead on Calumet—
before you reach the train.
We walk and we walk.

***

We are on the porch.
Lorraine says it's late but that time doesn't matter here.
Time is a circle.
Everything that has happened is happening right now.
On Earth, our minds can't comprehend,
but here, on the Other Side, time is tangible.
You can pick it up and play with it.

***

A Pertinent Question

Does being young, gifted, and Black
always mean die young?

I Can Be Sad in Public

It's a blessing
to lay oneself bare
and celebrate the mess.

List

after Lorraine Hansberry's List April 1, 1960

Things I'm Tired Of
My queerness
Boring conversation
Boring men
Boring women
Too many emails
Anxiety
Depression
My meds
Not taking my meds
Taking my meds
Wanting the Earth to stop
and let me off

Things I Like
Money
Cash
(These two are not always the same)
Lamictal
Wellbutrin
Men who take me seriously
Women who take me seriously
Being admired for my looks

Or

Does dying always feel so freeing or heavy?
Does dying always feel so freeing or heavy?
Does dying always feel so freeing or heavy?
Does dying always feel so freeing or heavy?
Does dying always feel so freeing or heavy?
Does dying always feel so freeing or heavy?
Does dying always feel so freeing or heavy?
Does dying always feel so freeing or heavy?
Does dying always feel so freeing or heavy?
Does dying always feel so freeing or heavy?
Does dying always feel so freeing or heavy?
Does dying always feel so freeing or heavy?
Does dying always feel so freeing or heavy?
Does dying always feel so freeing or heavy?
Does dying always feel so freeing or heavy?

In the End

I lost a friend

Through the door of no return.

Today she was alive.

It's dark.

If I meet you in the middle, we can double back.

I can take you with me.

Why do you have to go?

Time is a circle: I am here and she's there.

We should be able to meet in the middle.

Where is the somewhere that she is?

Can she catch a ride back?

What is the travel time?

Do we keep falling and falling and falling?

Where is the bottom? Can we leave? Does anyone get to go home?

If she's in the past

she's in the future

she is here too.

there is never goodbye.

acknowledgments

I'll start at the beginning: To my grandparents Eugene and Mildred Hill—thank you for encouraging me. My grandparents fostered my love for the written word and financially supported every enrichment program opportunity offered to me. My grandfather has passed on, but I know he's proud of me—wherever he is.

My introduction to poetry as a career came from my time in Oak Park & River Forest's Spoken Word Club. Thank you to Peter Khan and Dan Sullivan for the early support. Thank you to Young Chicago Authors teaching artists Tara Betts, Krista Franklin, and Toni Asante Lightfoot.

Thank you to Chicago poetry OG Patricia Smith.

Thank you to my favorite group chat: Eve Ewing, José Olivarez, Nate Marshall, and Fatimah Asghar. Thank you to my friends who held me down during grad school and beyond: Jessica Lynne, Hannah Giorgis, Doreen St. Felix, Melissa Centeno, Alexis Martin, Imani Brown, Atoosa Moinzadeh, Lisandra Bernadet, Boafoa Darko, Ikhlas Saleem, Allison Bland.

Thank you to my Pratt Institute Creative Writing MFA cohort—especially Mahogany L. Browne, Sasha Banks, Adrienna Greene, Lyric Hunter and our professors Christian Hawkey, Mendi Obadike, and James Hannaham.

Thank you to Ydalmi Noriega.

To my *Rookie* colleagues: Tavi Gevinson, Lena Singer, Derica Shields, and Lauren Redding.

Thank you to Peyton Morgan, Melody Morgan, and Hubert Morgan.

Thank you to my brother Rauland Sharp, my sister Joy Sharp, and my sister-in-law Aziza Sharp.

To my editor Maya Marshall.

Thank you to Rana Zoe Mungin who encouraged me to pursue an MFA. Zoe is no longer with us but I know she's somewhere out there laughing that glorious laugh of hers.

Thank you to Bassey Ikpi whose transparency helped me after my bipolar diagnosis. Thank you to Fatimah Warner for being a friend and providing a good soundtrack to my late-night writing.

I'd like to acknowledge Renina Jarmon who coined "Black Girls Are From the Future" and has a book by the same name.

The line "Bitch I'm taking calls, no small talk," which appears in my poem "Separation," comes from "Gahdamn" by Kari Faux ft. Childish Gambino.

Shout out to Solange for writing sad Black girl anthems.

If you have ever been a sad Black girl, this book is for you.

Thank you to the editors and journals who have published these poems in other venues and in earlier forms:

Winter Tangerine: "Hansberry & Cognac."

Lenny Letter: "Black Girls Are from the Future" and "Black Lady Lazarus."

BreakBeat Poets Vol: 2: Black Girl Magic: "Exile."

POETRY and *Respect the Mic: Celebrating 20 Years of Poetry from a Chicagoland High School:* "Super Sad Black Girl."

about the author

DIAMOND JANESE SHARP is a poet and essayist from Chicago. She has performed at Chicago's Stage 773 and her work has been featured on Chicago Public Radio. Her work has been published in *Vice*, *Pitchfork*, *Lenny*, *[PANK]*, *The Offing*, *Fjords*, *Winter Tangerine*, *JoINT Literary*, *Wellesley Review*, *Beltway Poetry Quarterly*, *Blackberry*, and elsewhere. A Callaloo fellow, Sharp is also a Wright/Hurston workshop participant and a member of the inaugural Poetry Foundation Incubator. Diamond is an associate editor of *Rookie* and an alumna of Wellesley College.

about haymarket books

Haymarket Books is a radical, independent, nonprofit book publisher based in Chicago. Our mission is to publish books that contribute to struggles for social and economic justice. We strive to make our books a vibrant and organic part of social movements and the education and development of a critical, engaged, international left.

We take inspiration and courage from our namesakes, the Haymarket martyrs, who gave their lives fighting for a better world. Their 1886 struggle for the eight-hour day—which gave us May Day, the international workers' holiday—reminds workers around the world that ordinary people can organize and struggle for their own liberation. These struggles continue today across the globe—struggles against oppression, exploitation, poverty, and war.

Since our founding in 2001, Haymarket Books has published more than five hundred titles. Radically independent, we seek to drive a wedge into the risk-averse world of corporate book publishing. Our authors include Noam Chomsky, Arundhati Roy, Rebecca Solnit, Angela Y. Davis, Howard Zinn, Amy Goodman, Wallace Shawn, Mike Davis, Winona LaDuke, Ilan Pappé, Richard Wolff, Dave Zirin, Keeanga-Yamahtta Taylor, Nick Turse, Dahr Jamail, David Barsamian, Elizabeth Laird, Amira Hass, Mark Steel, Avi Lewis, Naomi Klein, and Neil Davidson. We are also the trade publishers of the acclaimed Historical Materialism Book Series and of Dispatch Books.

also from haymarket books

Dear God. Dear Bones. Dear Yellow., Noor Hindi

The Body Family, Hope Wabuke

All the Blood Involved in Love, Maya Marshall

The Patron Saint of Making Curfew, Tim Stafford

Rifqa, Mohammed El-Kurd

There Are Trans People Here, H. Melt

I Remember Death by Its Proximity to What I Love, Mahogany L. Browne

Mama Phife Represents, Cheryl Boyce-Taylor

Milagro, Penelope Allegria

Lineage of Rain, Janel Pineda

Too Much Midnight, Krista Franklin

BreakBeat Poets Vol. 4: LatiNEXT, eds. Felicia Rose Chavez, José Olivarez, and Willie Perdomo

Can I Kick It?, Idris Goodwin

Build Yourself a Boat, Camonghne Felix

Citizen Illegal, José Olivarez

Black Queer Hoe, Britteney Black Rose Kapri